CANDLE WHIMSY

23 Bold, Bendy Projects That Break the Mold

ANNA DYKHOFF

Photography by Christoffer Dalkarls

Other Schiffer Craft Books on Related Subjects:

Creating Smudge Sticks: 15 Projects to Remove Negative Energy and Promote Wellness, Peg Couch, ISBN 978-0-7643-5999-6

The Graphic Guide to Beekeeping: Your Complete Visual Resource for Sweet Success, Yves Gustin, ISBN 978-0-7643-6124-1

How to Create Encaustic Art: A Guide to Painting with Wax, Birgit Hüttemann-Holz, ISBN 978-0-7643-5416-8

Originally published as *Ljus* by Natur & Kultur, Stockholm © 2023 by Anna Dykhoff
Translated from the Swedish by Carol Rhoades

Library of Congress Control Number: 2025939987

Photography by Christoffer Dalkarls
Front cover design by Lindsay Hess
Back cover design by Lori Malkin Ehrlich
Interior design by Sebastian Wadsted
Type set in Karl ST / Quadraat OT

ISBN: 978-0-7643-7137-0
ePub: 978-1-5073-0696-3
Printed in India

10 9 8 7 6 5 4 3 2 1

Published by Schiffer Craft
An imprint of Schiffer Publishing, Ltd.
4880 Lower Valley Road
Atglen, PA 19310
Phone: (610) 593-1777; Fax: (610) 593-2002
Email: Info@schifferbooks.com
Web: www.schifferbooks.com

CONTENTS

Getting Started

Liquid and warm, matte and smooth, thin and flexible. Candle wax has so many characteristics. It's a changeable and living material that can transform before our eyes. It softens with heat until it melts; at room temperature, it firms up again. The wax follows a set of rules—we have learned them so well that they have become a part of our culture.

Can wax also become a sculptural material to use the way we use clay or glass? What do the shapes we see in the workspace for handmade candles tell us about wax as a material? A candle workshop encompasses a whole world of rich handcraft traditions and stories conveying the meaning of candles for people over time.

Living light has been an absolute necessity for people's everyday life, but it's also been something elevated, festive, exclusive, and even holy. Use candlelight for a romantic dinner, blow out a candle so you'll get a wish, light a candle for someone who has gone away. Certain candles have always been reserved for particular occasions, and some of the materials were, in times past, available only to the wealthy. Today, candles are no longer something we depend on to light up the darkness, but even so, we consume an enormous amount. In my home country, Sweden, we use more candles than people elsewhere—46,000 tons of candles are used in Sweden every year. By experimenting with materials and techniques, I hope that I can raise questions about sustainability in relation to daily consumption of candles and, at the same time, provide access to the handcraft for more people.

The projects here are a mixture. They teach you traditional candles and creative new interpretations of them, because I hope to present wax in a way that encourages your own research into what's possible.

In my work I use wax's special characteristics to create unusual shapes and functions. I'll teach you various techniques for dipping, casting, and building with beeswax, and for dyeing wax. Along the way, you'll learn about this creative and sensuous material.

A Bit of Candle History

The significance of humans learning how to light up the darkness with the help of candles cannot be overestimated. The oldest known evidence of stearin used for lighting goes back to ancient Egypt. Archeological finds have uncovered remains of items similar to candles, produced with a combination of tallow and stearin. Those candles were used in the fourth century BCE.

The use of stearin for candle making continued through history, with increasing importance during the Middle Ages and Renaissance. However, for the general public, tallow and wax candles were clearly more common and more available. Tallow was often used as the primary raw material for making candles at home. But tallow candles burned dirty and produced soot; they dripped, and they smelled bad.

The expensive stearin that produced straight and smooth candles that burned cleanly, without soot or dripping, became highly sought after but were reserved for use in places such as churches and monasteries and, of course, for use by well-off people who had the means to buy expensive things.

During the nineteenth century, major advances occurred in research on fats and fatty acids. Research by Michel-Eugène Chevreul, a French chemist, resulted in new insights into stearin's characteristics. That increased knowledge about it allowed possibilities for more consistent and standardized production. Stearin candle making became industrialized, which led to the stearin candles we recognize today—easily available and cheap.

Materials

The candles sold in stores and shops seldom list the contents, but sometimes we see "100% stearin" stated on the packaging, or sometimes that the candle is made of paraffin. We rarely learn the origin of any listed materials. A few years ago, I knew very little about where the materials in the candles I bought came from or how that affected my surrounding environment and climate. But it became natural to dig into the questions when I began to buy materials for my own candle making.

In this book, and in my own making, I primarily use two basic materials: stearin and beeswax. The reason is that both stearin and beeswax are renewable raw materials with little effect on the climate—if you do your research and make conscious choices.

Stearin enables the beeswax to hold color differently and adjusts its hardness. Stearin is sometimes produced from slaughter waste, leavings from the meat industry, and other animal byproducts. Stearin may also be vegan, if extracted from vegetable oils such as palm oil or soy oil.

Many aspects of the animal, soy, and palm oil industries use resources unsustainably, causing great harm to the environment, so it's important to research your stearin's origins. There are various certifications that verify the sustainability of the material; one example is Svanen brand in the Nordic countries. If you don't see any certification, I recommend that you research the stearin producer and read about their approach to sourcing and manufacturing. It can be difficult to find the information, but if you don't see it online, ask about it! If enough of us ask questions, the information will, we can hope, become more readily available. What I'm looking for is a plant stearin produced from waste, or from sustainably produced vegetable oil.

The same goes for beeswax: Make sure it comes from a sustainable bioculture that sustains the bees' survival and contributes to the preservation of pollinators. Beeswax is the bees' building material, used to build the hive that protects the bees from outside impacts and dangers. In sustainable bioculture, the beeswax is harvested carefully in a way that doesn't hurt or stress the bees.

I decided to omit paraffin from this book because it is a byproduct of the petroleum fossil fuel industry. The extraction of paraffin is also a step in oil refining, a process that, in itself, is very energy consuming. An additional reason is the huge damage that paraffin does to the environment—burning of both petroleum and paraffin releases masses of greenhouse gases. Many environmental organizations are requesting that businesses phase out paraffin candles, because the damage occurs at large scale and a change there would make a big difference. For every ton of paraffin candles replaced by candles of renewable raw materials, we could count on avoiding a corresponding 3.14 tons of fossil carbon dioxide, according to the environmentally friendly brand Svanen. But, of course, we can make a difference in little ways—choose renewable raw materials for your candles and you've done something good!

The most common wick, and I use it in my candles, is a flat cotton wick, which you can buy in hobby shops. There are various thicknesses, usually indicated by numbers between 5 and 35. That size number is preceded by letters, which indicate the type of wick. The usual sizes are between 8 and 15; for a typical taper, a size 10 wick is common. For a larger-diameter candle—for example, a molded candle—you can go up to a size 12 or 15. Always do test burns with your wicks to ensure you choose the correct wick size for each specific candle: it must burn evenly without much soot and with a small, safe flame. Trimming the wick to about ¼ in. (6 mm) before lighting it also helps to ensure that your candle burns safely.

MEHILÄISVAHA, VALKAISTU
0301-1018-2032
BEE'S WAX, BLEACHED
1,5 kg
KYMIN PALOKÄRKI - PORVOO
Tillsätt färgen i varm ljusmassa
(ca 85°C) och rör om väl till dess
all färg löst sig.
Räcker till ca 1kg
ljus- eller gjutmassa.
Tillsätt färgen i varm ljusmassa
(ca 85gr C) och rör om väl till
dess all färg löst sig
Räcker till ca 1kg ljus- eller
gjutmassa
Joel Svenssons Vaxfabrik AB

max. 2100 W

Tools

You don't actually need any specialized tools to begin making your own candles. You probably already have most of what you need at home! To melt wax, you need a stovetop, a saucepan, a digital kitchen scale, and a container for melting wax in. The container can be a small one purchased in a store's candle-making supply section, or it can be a glass jar, such as a recycled jam jar. Avoid using plastic because it can melt or lose its shape in the warm-water bath.

Speaking of nonspecialized tools: Wooden skewers are my most used tools when it comes to candle making. I use them for everything—to stir what's in the melting container, to tie wicks to, to center the wick in molds, and more. Skewers are my duct tape; you can solve almost anything with them!

All the items you use, not only containers and pots but every tool, will eventually get wax on it, so think about that when you choose your equipment, even though it's true you can clean them completely with some scrubbing and warm water. My landlord was understandably unhappy when I used his saucepan for melting wax. (I'm sorry, Baris!) It can be worthwhile to have a saucepan just for your candle projects—buy one at a flea market.

When you are dipping, you'll need a place to set the skewers that the candles hang on while they cool. One solution for keeping this efficient is to dip many candles at the same time and set up a sawhorse or folding rack with a couple of wooden strips. Space the strips on the rack so that the skewers you secured your wicks on can rest on them. It would help to fasten down the wooden strips with a clamp on each side—so you won't bump them and knock down all the newly dipped candles. An even quicker solution would be to hang your skewers between two chairbacks or on the edges of an empty, folded-narrower-as-needed cardboard carton.

A thermometer is necessary for controlling the temperature when melting wax. This is partly so the wax will behave as we want when we use it in a candle project, and partly for safety. The wax should not be warmer than around 160°F (70°C) when you work with it.

Beyond that, think about how to handle the warm melting container—keep at the ready some protective gloves or a kitchen towel you can sacrifice as a potholder so you won't burn yourself.

When you're working with sheets of beeswax, you should have a cutting mat or other protective surface and a good utility knife. Hello from someone who always manages to cut herself when the risk arises—be careful with sharp knives.

To cut uneven pieces off your candle, for example, to make a flat base so the candle can stand upright, it is best to use a warm knife. I use a hot-air gun, a tool that can be handy now and then for candle making, but it's not a necessity.

Finally, safety! This should be quite obvious: Never leave a burning candle unattended. This applies to all candles, but it is especially important with homemade candles because they may drip more than bought candles and because the shape of the candle can affect how it burns. Some shapes and wax experiments are better as decorative rather than functional candles and should, if lit, be burned only when very closely watched. Use your common sense, and always position your candles securely.

Also, remember that wax is a flammable material. Never let your wax reach unsafe temperatures. As you work, keep it away from flame and take care not to overheat it. If wax reaches its flash point and ignites, do *not* try to put out the fire with water: Always smother a wax fire. Use a pot lid, a damp towel, baking soda, or a correctly rated fire extinguisher.

max. 2100
Level
Temp.
Timer
Temp.
Timer
On / Standby

Melting the Wax

The easiest way to melt wax is in a water bath on the stovetop. Before you begin, however, you need to think about a few things.

You can buy special melting pots in a hobby shop, but, really, a glass canning jar or recycled jam jar or metal can works just as well. If you're going to dip into a pot, you need to consider the candle length to make sure it will fit into your container.

Once you have all your equipment, you can begin melting. Prepare the wax mixture in your melting pot. I use a 1-to-2 mix of beeswax and stearin; for example, a ratio of 100 grams (g) of beeswax to 200 g of stearin. Beeswax is softer than stearin and produces a nice smooth candle mass. Plus, it gives the candle a beautiful pale-golden color and a lovely honey scent. You can find bleached beeswax if you prefer a completely white candle, or if you want a color that is easier to mix from a white base.

How much wax you need depends on the size of the melting pot and the project you want to make. For a 1-pint (0.5 liter) jam jar, you can begin with 200 g beeswax and 400 g stearin, if no other amounts are specified in the instructions.

BASIC PROCEDURES

Set your melting pot with the wax in a water bath; that is, in a saucepan of water over medium heat.

When the wax melts, it sinks down, so if the wax didn't all fit in at first, you can add more as it melts. Stir now and then with, for example, a skewer to speed up the melting. You want to have an even and slow melting to avoid burning the wax, so take your time melting the wax. Plan on at least one hour, depending on how much wax you're melting.

If you're going to dip the candle, make sure you have enough melted wax in your pot so the entire length of the candle you want will be coated with the wax. Another method is to heat water in a new saucepan to the same temperature as the melted wax (about 160°F [70°C]), then pour it into your melting pot until the level of the water is an inch or so (a few centimeters) below the edge of the pot. The water can lie beneath the melted wax. This is a good alternative if you don't have much wax to melt, or if you want to dip with a new color or wax mixture and don't want to use a new pot for the test wax.

If you're going to cast candles, you need to make sure that you melt enough wax to fill the form you will be using. When your wax is completely melted, you should keep it at about 160°F (70°C) while you work on your candle project.

Don't pour wax down the sink, since that would create a lot of extra work (plumbing issues!). Instead, when you need to clean a saucepan you melted wax in, for example, work like this: Fill that saucepan with boiling water. Wait while the water cools and the wax has completely solidified and sticks to the surface. Then, all you have to do is to pick off the wax and reuse it.

Warm water lies below the melted wax in a dipping container.

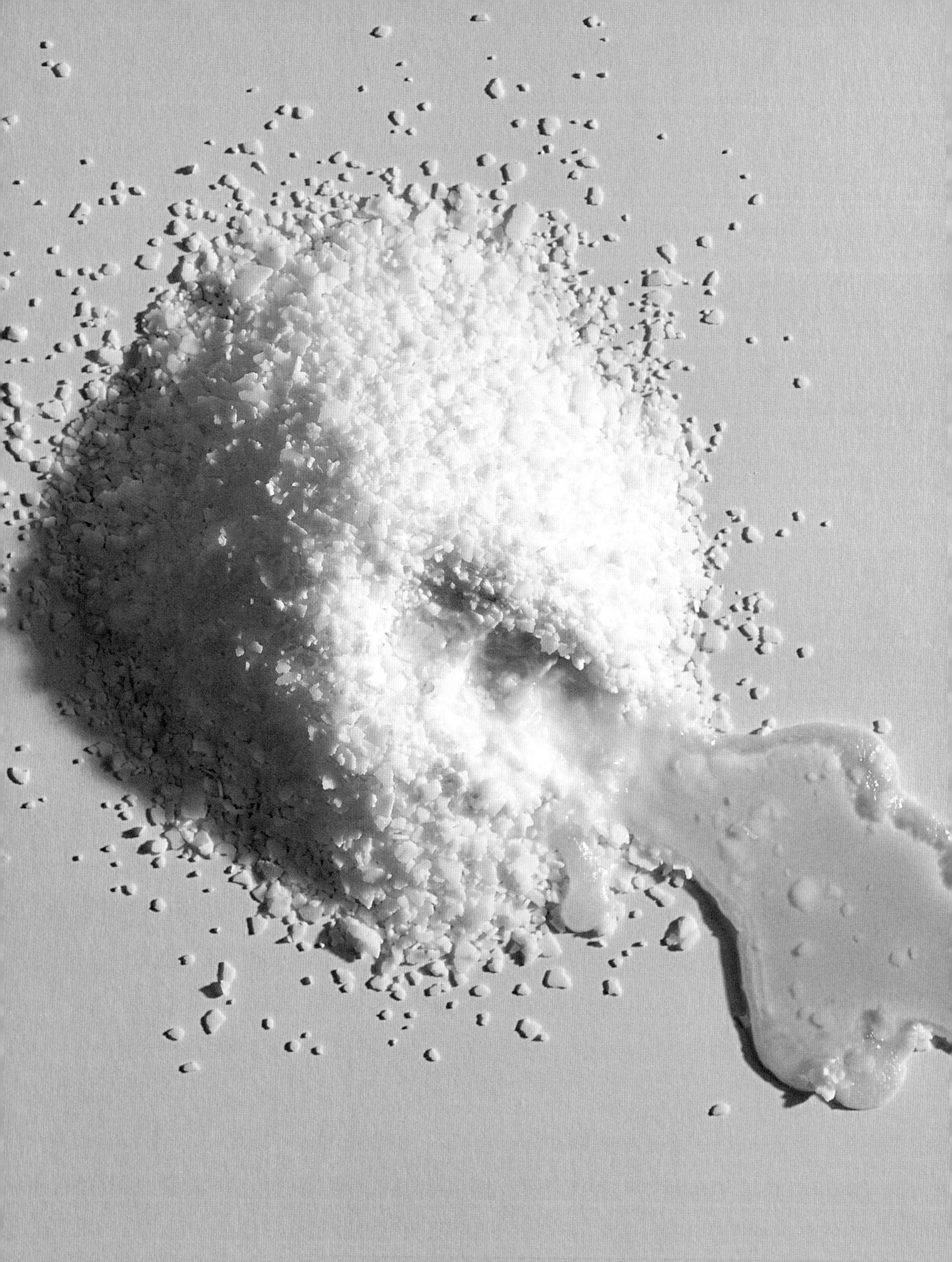

DIPPING

Dipping is the easiest technique for most people who want to try candle making. The taper candles we use today get their shape from dipping as a technique, even though most aren't made that way anymore but are cast in metal forms or shaped by a hydraulic press.

But hand-dipped candles have a special quality, and it's easy to achieve a nice form. Maybe that's why so many have tried candle dipping in school—it really is a handcraft anyone can do. A wick with a weight is dipped into the melted wax. When it hardens, it's dipped again to build up volume. Gravity gives the candle its conical shape.

Dipping is almost meditative for me. I can take a step back and let myself be led by the materials. That guides my repetitive movements and tells me when I am ready for each step in the process.

Dipped candles can have more than just a simple taper appearance. By working with the dipped items while they are still warm and flexible, you can bend and twist them—even around each other—so you can make a candle with a double or triple wick.

Branch candles, or multiarm candles, are also classic dipped candles made by sewing wicks of varying lengths together, which are then dipped and shaped afterward.

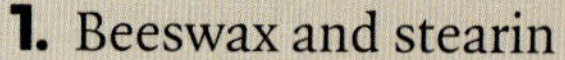

1. Beeswax and stearin
2. A weight pulls down and straightens the wick.
3. The wick has been dipped three times in the melted wax.
4. The wick dipped ten times
5. The wick dipped twenty times

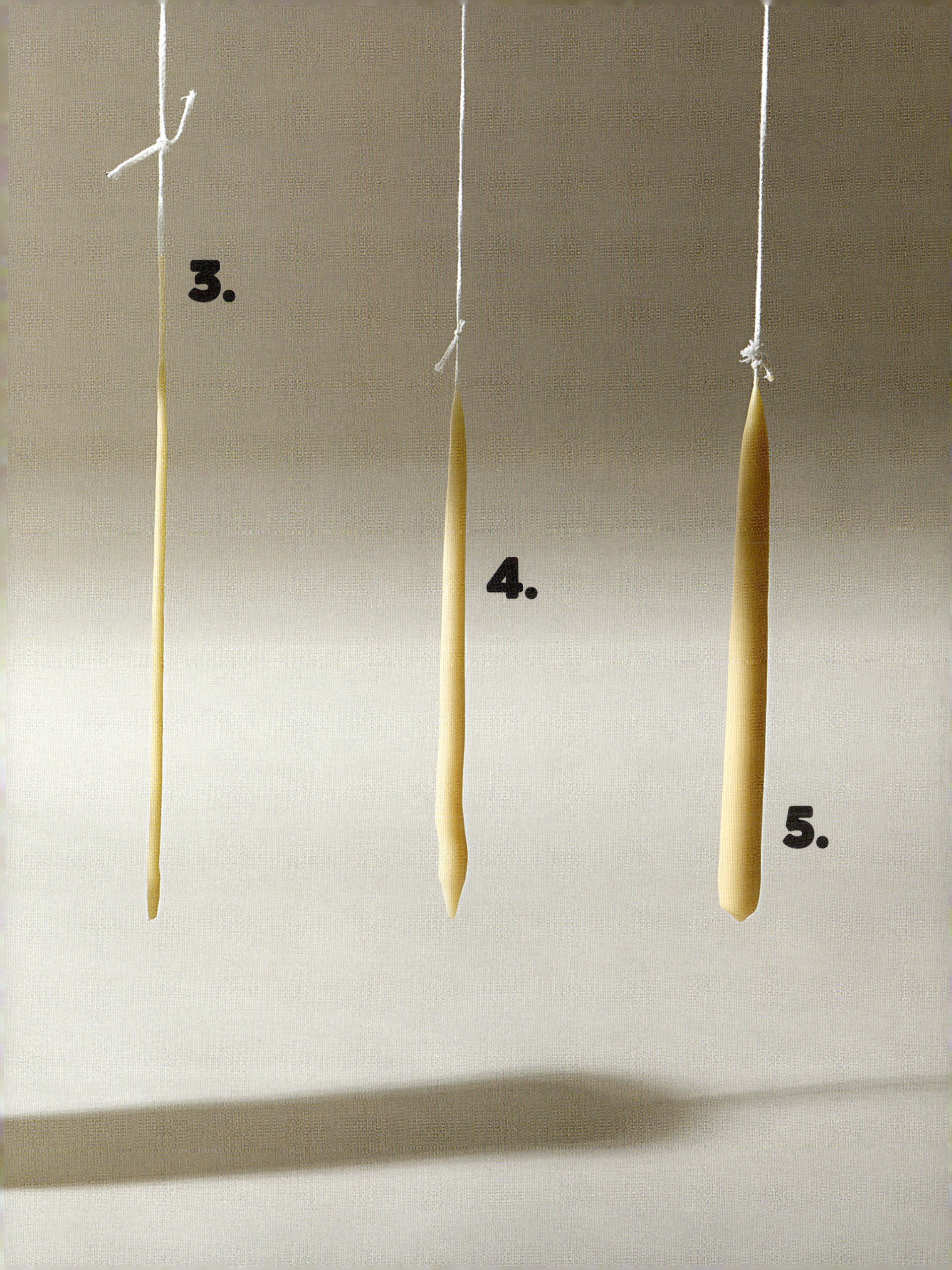
3.
4.
5.

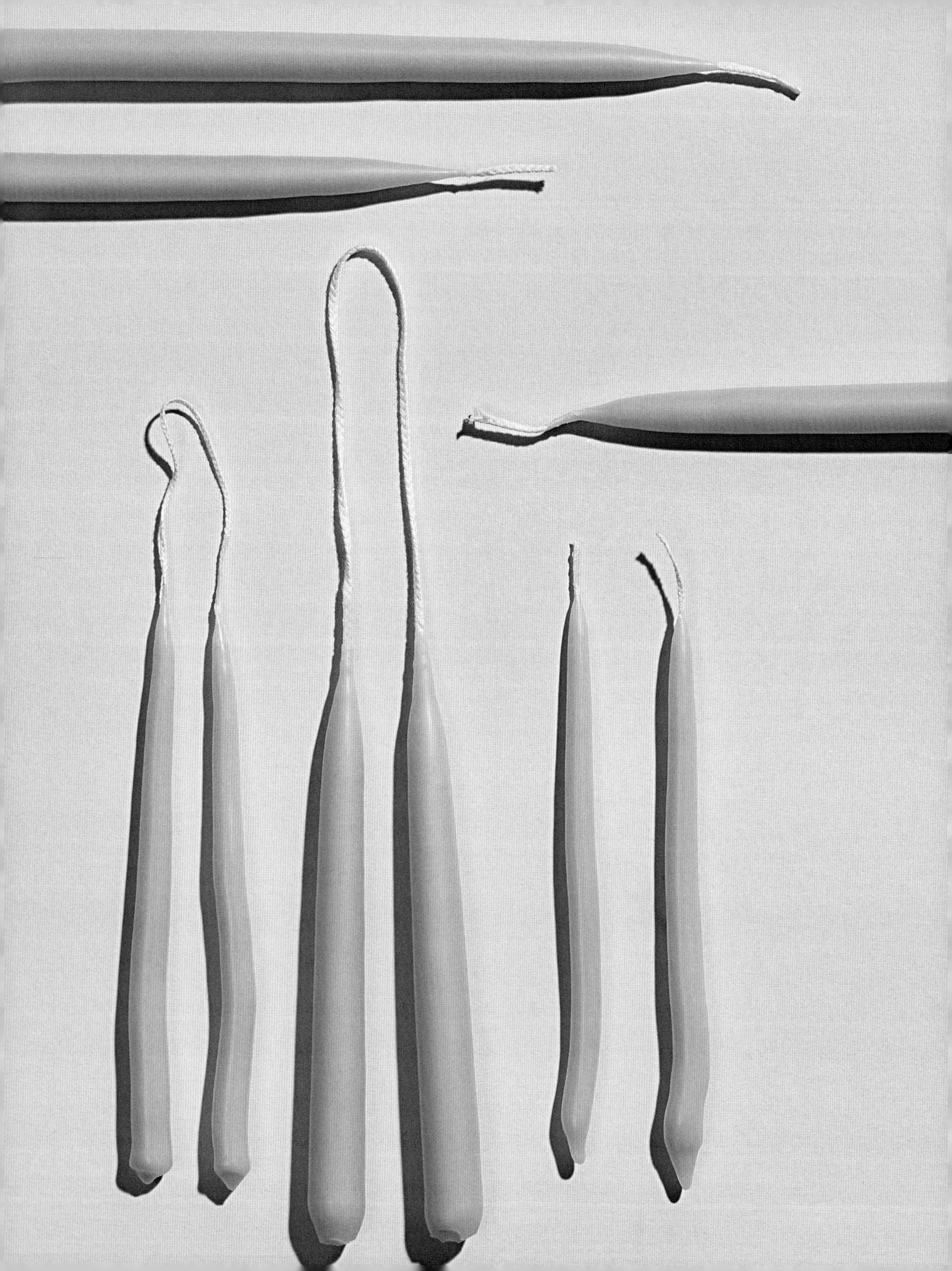

Taper Candle

A perfect first project for anyone new to candle making—the classic taper. A taper needs about twenty-five dips for a nice shape and a good size.

WHAT YOU NEED

- Wax mixture (see page 21)
- Kitchen scale
- Melting pot (tall enough for the candle length you want)
- Saucepan
- Thermometer
- Wick
- Small weight (a metal nut is perfect)
- Scissors
- Knife
- Wooden skewers or small sticks to tie the wicks to
- A place to hang the skewers with the candles while they dry (for example, between two chairs or racks)

Melt the wax, following the instructions on page 21.

While the wax melts, you can prepare the wicks. Cut them in either a double or single length in relation to the depth of the melting pot you will use, plus an inch or so (a few centimeters) for tying. Attach the wicks to the skewers. If you have a double length, you'll have two candles to join on the wick! Now securely tie a small weight on the end of each wick.

It's a good idea to make five to ten candles when you are using the dipping method. That's because the candles need to cool a bit between each dip. Having a set of candles ready to dip makes it easier to get a good rhythm going, so you won't have to stand and wait for each candle to solidify enough before you can dip it again.

Never let your wax reach unsafe temperatures! When the wax reaches a temperature of 160°F (70°C), it's time to dip! Dip the wick first until the weight goes down into the bottom of the melting pot, and keep the wick in the wax for about ten seconds. Pull the skewer up and let it drip off a bit before you hang it up in the drying spot you prepped. The remaining dips can be shorter—a couple of seconds—because the wax has hardened on the wick and won't melt away in the warm wax. If, after several dips, you think that wax has barely hardened on the wick, you can try lowering the heat a little or waiting a little longer between each dip.

The weight helps hold the candle straight, so, if you think the candles are still a little crooked, you can always straighten them while they are warm by carefully pulling on the wicks or bending the candles. After about ten dips, the candle should have enough stability to continue without the weight—you can cut it off and continue doing the rest of the dips without a weight.

When you've achieved the shape you want for your candles, all you have to do next is to cut away any drops from the base of each candle for a neat and stable finish. Now let the candles cool completely.

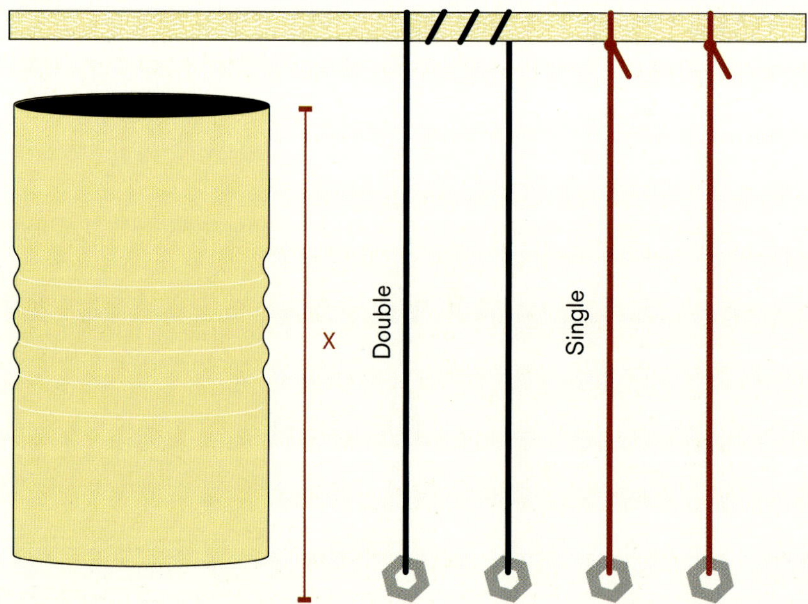

Spiral Candle

A sculptural candle is easy to make. By twisting the wick around a skewer while it's warm and then letting it harden, you'll shape a spiral. Then, all you have to do is to dip the candle as usual.

WHAT YOU NEED

- Wax mixture (see page 21)
- Kitchen scale
- Melting pot (tall enough for the candle length you want)
- Saucepan
- Thermometer
- Wick
- Some dowels or rods about ⅝–1¼ in. (1.5–3 cm) in diameter
- Wooden skewers or small sticks to tie the wicks to
- Scissors
- Knife
- A place to hang the skewers with the candles while they dry (for example, between two chairs or racks)

Melt the wax, following the instructions on page 21.

While the wax melts, cut the wick in a double length in relation to the melting pot you will use. To begin with, the wick does not have to be secured to a skewer, so start with a loose wick. Make a slipknot on one end of each wick, so it will be easy to attach it onto a skewer or stick after you've shaped it.

When the wax has melted, dip the wick in for about ten seconds. Have the dowel or rod ready. Take up the wick and, while it is still soft, twist the wick around the rod. When the wick has been rolled around the rod and is no longer dripping, set it down to dry completely. While it dries, you can continue with the next wick: Dip and twist, set down to dry.

Once the wick has dried on the rod, loosen it carefully and pry it away from the rod. Now you can attach the wick to a skewer or stick for the remaining dips. The second and third dips need to be rather quick, so that the heat from the melted wax doesn't loosen the wax away from the wick too much, causing it to lose its shape. If that happens, you'll just have to twist the wick around the rod again. You should wait a few minutes between the initial dips, so that the wick hardens properly in its twisted shape. Then, continue dipping until the candle has the shape you like. Finish by trimming away any drops on the base so the candle will be stable. Let the candle cool completely.

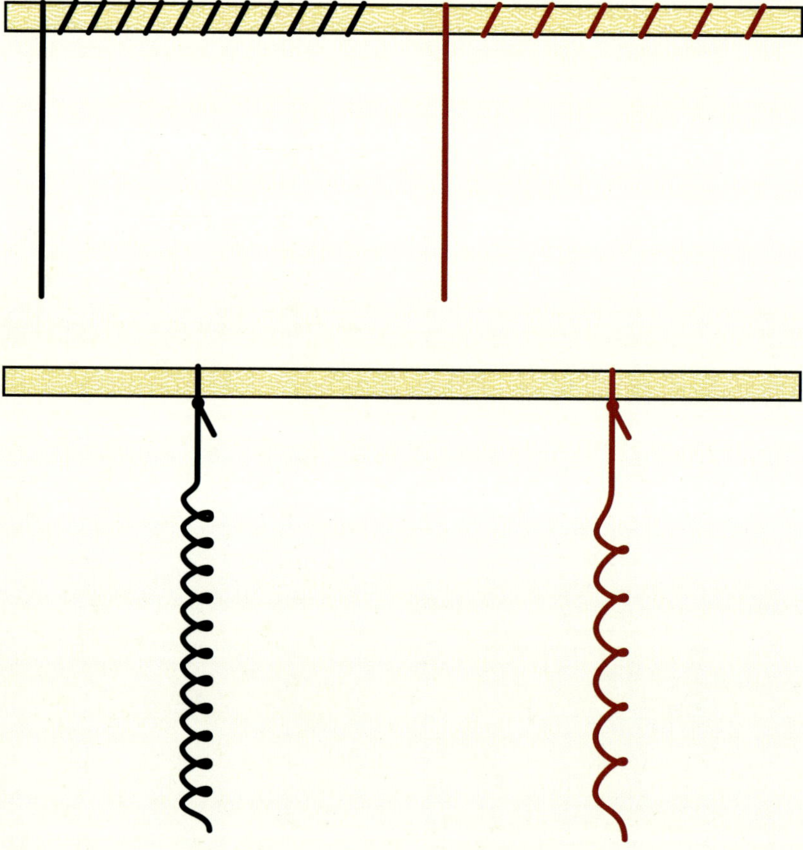

Candle Crown

Dipping a candle with a steel wire base and a wick is a classic technique. People have long dipped candles to make an impressive centerpiece or wear like a crown. This candle is somewhat more irregular than its forebears, but the technique is basically the same.

WHAT YOU NEED

- Wax mixture (see page 21)
- Kitchen scale
- Melting pot (tall enough for the candle length you want)
- Saucepan
- Thermometer
- Wick
- Steel wire
- Wire cutters
- Scissors
- Knife
- Wooden skewers or small sticks to tie the wicks to
- Heatproof pad to dry candle crown on

Melt the wax, following the instructions on page 21. Use a dipping pot tall enough for the candle length you want.

Begin by shaping the base of the candle crown. Snip off a piece of steel wire about 15¾ in. (40 cm) long. Fold it at the middle and make an eyelet loop by twisting the wire around itself. Continue the same way until you have a row of loops. You can also try other ways to make the loops—begin at one end of the wire, bend it into a loop, and twist it around itself.

When you've twisted a few bits, four or five pieces, you can begin to assemble them into a larger piece. Twist them together at the ends and use smaller pieces of wire to wrap them together.

Start by considering the shape, height, and diameter of your crown. If you want a cylindrical shape that is even overall, make a strip in the

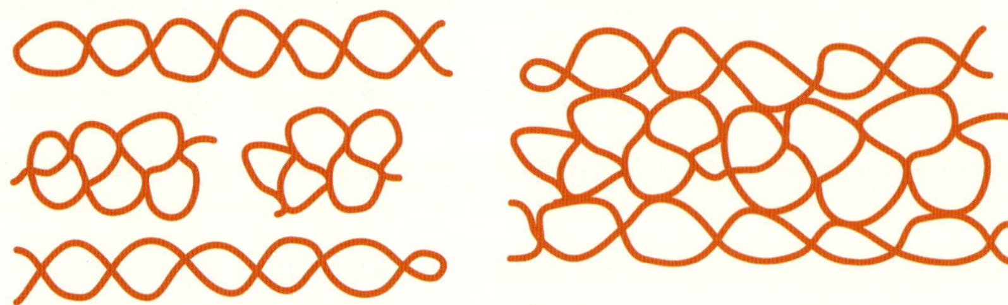

same length as the circumference you want. Bend it into a circle and wrap the short ends together. If, instead, you want your candle crown to be bell or cone shaped, you can build up your pieces and form them until they are a shape you are satisfied with.

Once you've finished the base of the candle crown, it's time to attach the wicks for the candles in the crown. Think about how many candles you want and where you want to place them on the crown. Plan to space each wick about an inch or so (a few centimeters) apart so they can all burn safely. Tie the wicks firmly to the base. Attach the wicks to the skewers and make sure you can hold the crown so it stays straight as you dip. This is a little tricky, but it is worthwhile to make sure that everything hangs straight.

Before you begin dipping the crown, I recommend that you wrap the wick yarn around the steel wire on the base. This makes it easier for the wax to adhere to the base. I've learned that dipping directly onto the steel wire takes quite a while longer because the wax can't harden as quickly on metal, which, in turn, makes it harder to produce an evenly thick layer of wax over the entire crown. You don't need to wrap the wick especially tightly around the wire, but just make sure that it is evenly divided over the entire base.

Now it's time to dip! Besides making sure that the crown hangs straight, there are no other big challenges to dipping a candle crown. There are a few things to consider, though: If you notice that the wax is building up more slowly on the base than on the wicks while you dip, you can simply dip the base in a few times more until there is an even thickness all over. Because the liquid wax runs off the form, it can take a bit of time to build up the wax on the top of the form. Be sure to let the crown cool down properly between dips, so the wax will build up more evenly over the entire form.

When you're satisfied with the shape of your candle crown, trim the drops from the bottom so it will stand evenly. As with all candles, keep your eyes on it when it's lit, and make sure it's on a tray or base that won't be damaged by heat or drips.

Branch Candle

This three-armed candle is a traditional Christmas candle in some cultures, but I think it can be set out year round. The shape is definitely ceremonious and festive! A little challenge with this candle is getting an even thickness. So the candle branching won't be too narrow where the wicks meet, the candle needs to cool properly between each dip.

WHAT YOU NEED

- Wax mixture (see page 21)
- Kitchen scale
- Melting pot (tall enough for the candle length and, in this case, the width you want)
- Saucepan
- Thermometer
- Ruler, thumb stick, or measuring tape
- Large-eyed (tapestry) needle
- Wick
- Small weight (a metal nut is perfect!)
- Scissors
- Knife
- Wooden skewers or small sticks to tie the wicks to
- A place to hang the skewers with the candles while they dry (for example, between two chairs or racks)

Melt the wax, following the instructions on page 21.

While the wax melts, prepare the wicks. Cut one wick 18¼ in. (46 cm) long and one 15¾ in. (40 cm) long. Thread the shorter wick into the needle. This will be the vertical wick for the candle. Fold the longer wick at the middle so you have a center point. This wick will build the outer branches of the candle. Insert the short wick into the center point of the long wick.

Now you can tie the wicks onto a skewer. Begin with the two outermost wicks. Securely tie them spaced about 8 in. (20 cm) apart. Then, firmly knot the middle wick centered between the two outer wicks. Tie a weight at the end of the middle wick.

Because this candle needs to cool thoroughly between each dip, I recommend that you make a few of them at the same time. That way, you'll develop a good rhythm when you dip them, and they can cool before you come back to them for the next dip.

Once you've tied the candle to the skewer and the wax has melted completely, it's time to dip. Begin by dipping the wicks without shaping them—let the weight do the job. After five to eight dips, you can cut the weight off. Once you've dipped the candle, let it cool until it no longer drips. Set it on a tabletop and carefully shape the outer wicks into a branch form. When you do that, you'll need to move the outer knot points a bit closer to the center. You can shape the candle as you dip it. It's not a problem if it breaks a little while it is still thin. You can melt it together when you dip it again. If the candle becomes even narrower where the branches meet, it's not a big problem since it won't affect how the candle burns.

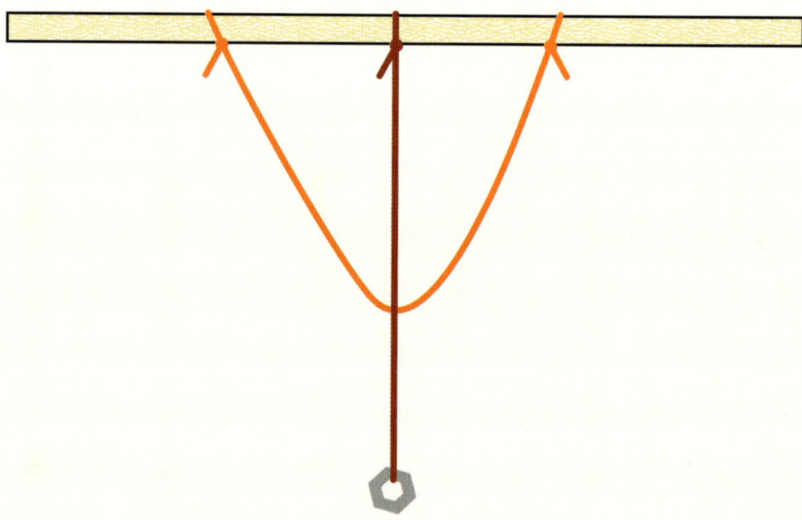

BUILDING AND SHAPING

Forming candles with beeswax is a method that can be very quick and easy, but it also offers possibilities for producing more-complex shapes. It's my favorite method and the one I've spent the most time on in my candle making.

Beeswax sheets are pretty in themselves with their geometric pattern and golden-yellow color. A classic rolled beeswax candle is wonderful in its simple construction. You can also dip them into melted wax, something that completely changes the look. It gives the impression that the candle is dipped or molded, but generally it is faster to make a dipped beeswax-sheet candle than to make a candle in a mold. You'll also be freer to play with shapes than when you dip on a single wick.

Dipping these in wax is my innovation and something I have not actually seen anywhere else. Possibly there's some candlemaker shaking her head at the idea when she reads this. But I think it's so rewarding, a quick and fun method for sculpting shapes in wax. When the candle later burns, melts down, and reveals the core of beeswax sheet, it tells us something about the characteristics of the wax. I personally think it's great to experience as an invitation to the process behind it.

When you work with beeswax, you can think of it as a material like clay, which can be shaped with your hands, simply adopting organic forms. You can also think of it as being like wood, in that you can build something from multiple pieces.

2.
1.
3.

1. Beeswax sheets and wick
2. Rolled forms
3. Forms built together
4. Dipping
5. Finished candle
4.
5.

Rolled Beeswax Candle

This is the easiest candle you can make—the only thing you need is a sheet of beeswax and a length of wick. Even the simplest techniques provide a wealth of possibilities. You can easily create a large variety of rolled beeswax candles: Try cutting a beeswax sheet into a shape before you roll it; dip it in beeswax; dye the wick; or use a hot air gun to shape the candle. Or just let the material speak for itself, as it does in this simple, rolled candle.

WHAT YOU NEED

- Beeswax sheets
- Wick
- Scissors
- Knife

Cut the wick so it is somewhat longer than your beeswax sheet. Lay the wick about ⅛ in. (a few millimeters) inside the edge of the beeswax sheet and begin rolling the sheet around the wick. Try to roll the beeswax around the wick as tightly as possible, so the candle will be stable and straight. Continue rolling the sheet around the wick until the candle is the diameter you want.

Rolled Beeswax Candle with a Foot

A rolled beeswax candle with its encircling foot can stand on its own. The beeswax is malleable as long as it is warm. A warm summer's day guarantees malleability. On a cold day in my workshop in the garage, I need the help of a heating fan so the wax won't crack. You may use a hairdryer.

The softness of the beeswax offers many possibilities for making something fun—can you sculpt a knot? An encircling base that stretches along the whole table? Maybe two, three, or four rolled candles meeting in a common tangle?

WHAT YOU NEED

- Beeswax sheets
- Wicks
- Scissors
- Knife

IF YOU'RE GOING TO DIP THE CANDLE, YOU ALSO NEED

- Wax mixture (see page 21)
- Melting pot
- Saucepan
- Thermometer

If you plan on dipping the candle, begin by melting the wax, following the instructions on page 21.

Make a simple rolled candle by following the instructions for the rolled beeswax candle on page 51, but make it a little longer so it is also long enough to form the ring foot.

Carefully bend the roll so it doesn't split or break. A hairdryer, hot-air gun, or heating fan is a good help if your wax feels brittle and might easily break. Heat the wax for a little while so it's more malleable. Then all you have to do is shape the encircling foot. Work on a flat surface such as a tabletop so the candle will stand up steady.

When you dip the candle, it's best to let it dry standing on a protected tabletop, so it will maintain its shape. Dip the candle until the beeswax sheet is no longer visible. Take into consideration that the wax hardens more slowly on the outside of the form because it runs off in liquid form. If you notice it's difficult for the wax to build up on the outside of the foot, you can turn the candle when you take it out of the dipping pot, so the wax will run in another direction before it hardens. Another tip is to let the candle cool completely between each dip, so that the wax that has hardened on the candle doesn't melt away when you dip the next time. When you are satisfied with the shape of the candle, cut away any drops from the bottom so you'll have a neat finish.

Beesswax Candle Crown

Because it's so malleable, beeswax is easy to shape into small structures.

WHAT YOU NEED

- Beeswax sheets
- Wick
- Steel wire
- Scissors
- Knife
- Wire cutters

IF YOU'RE GOING TO DIP THE CANDLE, YOU ALSO NEED

- Wax mixture (see page 21)
- Melting pot
- Saucepan
- Thermometer
- Wooden skewers or another type of small stick to tie wicks to

Roll three candles, following the instructions for rolling out beeswax on page 51. Roll a beeswax sheet with a wick. Carefully begin bending the roll without a wick. Bend it into a circle and join the ends. It should be sufficient just to clamp the ends and pinch the roll together. Now arrange the rolled candles evenly spaced inside the circle. Join the candles and base with a length of steel wire so it sits properly. Just insert a short piece of steel wire through each candle and into the base.

If you plan on dipping the candle, securely tie the wicks on to skewers, making sure you can hold the candle straight while you dip. It is easiest to let this candle dry on a protected tabletop. You'll notice that the wax does not build up as quickly on the outside of the form. This is because the wax runs off as liquid. Let the candle cool well between each dip, to make it easier to build up the wax on the outside of the candle. When you are satisfied with your candle, trim off any uneven bits and make sure it sits flat before you let it cool completely.

Ball Candle

This technique makes it easy to sculpt soft, organic forms for your candles. It's also super quick!

The process for this candle is one of my favorites. It's an obvious shape that is still quite playful.

Did you cut some sheet beeswax for the half-in-half gherkin candle on page 64? Take the leftovers and hand-mold a ball candle with them.

WHAT YOU NEED

- Beeswax, whole sheet or leftover bits
- Wick

IF YOU'RE GOING TO DIP THE CANDLE, YOU ALSO NEED

- Wax mixture (see page 21)
- Melting pot
- Saucepan
- Thermometer
- Knife
- Scissors
- Wooden skewers or another type of small stick to tie wicks to
- A place to hang the skewer with the candle while it dries (for example, between two chairs or book stacks)

If you plan on dipping the candle, begin by melting the wax, following the instructions on page 21.

While the wax melts, cut a wick to the length you want for your candle plus an inch or so (a few centimeters) extra. Press the beeswax sheet bits directly onto the wick—take small bits of wax and mash them onto the wick and into each other. Mold the wax into small balls on the wick. When you're happy with the shapes, you can either dip them or use them as is. Just make sure that the balls hold together so the candle will stand upright and steady.

If you're going to dip the candle, tie it to a small stick and make sure you've prepped a spot to hang it while it dries. Dip the candle in the melted wax until the beeswax sheet is no longer visible. Trim off any drops from the bottom so you'll have a neat finish.

Hand-molded beeswax candles can take on many more shapes than balls. For example, you can hand-mold a candle crown or combine various shapes into a stack, or make a shapeless clump more like a block candle in its dimensions. This is absolutely an easy and rewarding technique!

I placed the candles shown on page 58 in blue candleholders I made of wax (see also page 114).

Half-in-Half Gherkin Candle

I adapted this technique from furniture making, with a strong and versatile joint that I've used when making stools, sculptures, and tables. For this application, I used it to quickly transform two-dimensional sheet beeswax into three dimensions—a technique that opens up the options for many different forms. This pickle candle was named by a classmate who referred to it as an abstract fruit. I think it's an appropriate description.

WHAT YOU NEED

- Beeswax, whole sheet or leftover bits
- Wick
- Knife
- Scissors
- Cutting mat
- Steel ruler

IF YOU'RE GOING TO DIP THE CANDLE, YOU ALSO NEED

- Wax mixture (see page 21)
- Melting pot
- Saucepan
- Thermometer
- Wooden skewers or another type of small stick to tie wicks to
- A place to hang the skewer with the candle while it dries (for example, between two chairs or book stacks)

If you plan on dipping the candle, begin by melting the wax, following the instructions on page 21.

This candle consists of two halves joined together, and each half has four layers of beeswax sheet. You'll need to cut out four identical shapes from the beeswax sheet for each half: a total of eight pieces per candle. For my candles, I varied the shapes for the two halves somewhat. Begin by cutting the pieces. Take inspiration from a pickle or some other shape—see above for some suggestions!

Next, cut the wick somewhat longer than your cut shapes. Add an inch or so (a few centimeters) extra to the wick and even more for tying up if you are going to dip the candle.

Stack the same-shaped pieces four high, using two stacks per candle. Decide which is the top and bottom of the pieces, and arrange them so they're upright.

Take two stacks of pieces the same shape and make a ¼ in. wide (0.5 cm) slit in the middle of the forms—from the lower edge up to the center. Next, cut an equal-width slit in each of the other two stacks, but from the top edge down to the center. Take the two stacks cut from the top down and place the wick in the middle of one form. Then lay the other stack on top so the wick is fixed in the middle.

Now take the other two stacks and slide them into the cuts. The wick should be centered, so begin by adjusting one section on one side of the wick before you place the other section on the other side. Now the wick is centered in the candle, and the pieces should be joined so they are aligned on their top and bottom edges.

Clamp the joint so it doesn't gap anywhere. If you're going to dip the candle, first tie the wick to a skewer and begin dipping when the wax mixture is completely melted. Dip until the beeswax sheet is no longer visible. Trim off any drops from the bottom to make sure your candle will stand upright and steady.

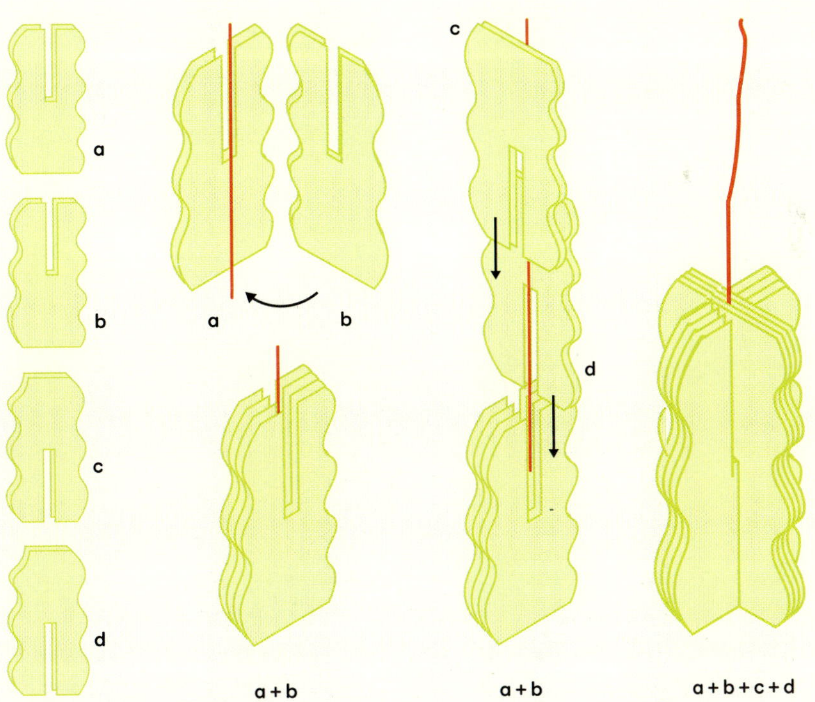

Combined Techniques

These simple techniques—rolling, sculpting, and half-in-half—pave the way for so many projects and applications. I encourage you to really experiment with these techniques and also to combine them in different ways. Try stacking various elements on each other.

What happens when a rolled beeswax candle has a molded foot added on? When the architectural half-in-half construction has a shapeless top? When a pair of rolled beeswax candles meet in a clumpy plinth? When a half-in-half construction becomes the base for a rolled beeswax candle?

For some combinations of shapes, it's easier to build the form first and then draw the wick through, using a large-eyed needle, while others can be sculpted directly on the wick.

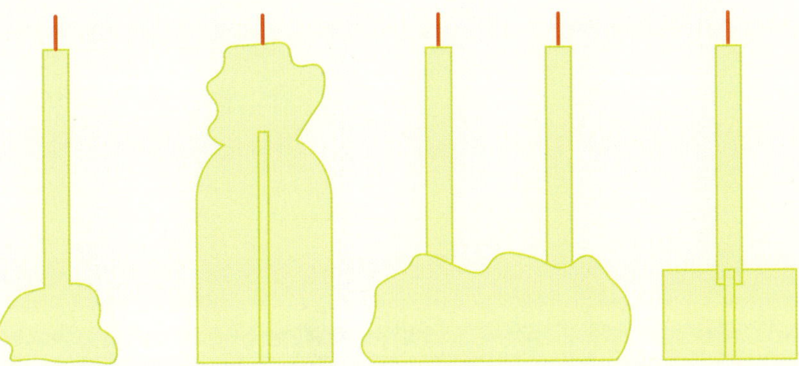

CASTING

The process of casting has something especially magic about it. Pouring the wax into the mold, watching it slowly harden from the outside in, and coming back after a while to release the result is always exciting. Preparing a mold can be as easy as punching a hole in a milk carton, using a clay original, making a silicone mold, or even making a 3-D-printed mold.

A well-made mold gives you a reliable method for producing several examples of the same shape. Using liquid silicone allows you to capture the shape of an object or a mold of its negative shape, to then mold it as positive in wax. The shape can be a pretty stone, something found at a flea market, a fruit, a 3-D-printed shape, or some wood blocks you nailed together. Silicone can pick up the smallest little detail for fun and special effects in the final candle.

An even simpler mold can be found in the recycling bin—milk cartons, toilet paper tubes, soda cans, or juice boxes also make good molds. Wax usually easily slips off materials such as plastic and metal. I seldom use any substance for releasing the wax. However, if the mold has a more complex form, or a form with a lot of texture, I recommend spraying it with a release material that you can buy in a hobby shop, or just lightly coating the mold with oil. It is so discouraging to have made an effort with a mold only to return to it, cooled, with the candle completely stuck in it so you have to melt out the wax. Doing a little test before you cast a finished candle is a good idea!

I've also experimented with molding in sand; you can see the results in the "Ideas and Experiments" chapter (pages 107–122).

2.
1.

1. Materials for casting
2. Stone for a mold
3. Casting in a silicone mold
4. Finished candle

Casting in a Soda Can

Here's a block candle molded in a common aluminum soda can. A metal mold yields a sleek, smooth surface. If you want to play with the form, you can manipulate the can before you mold in it!

WHAT YOU NEED

- Wax mixture (see page 21)
- Kitchen scale
- Melting pot
- Saucepan
- Thermometer
- Wick
- Soda can
- Hacksaw
- Scissors
- Knife
- Drill with a small-gauge drill bit (or an awl)
- Duct tape
- Wooden skewer or a similar little stick to center the wick

Melt the wax, following instructions on page 21.

Prepare the can: Use the hacksaw to saw off the top of the can or cut it off with a knife. Watch out because the raw edge is sharp!

Turn the can upside down and drill a small hole about 1⁄16 in. (2 mm) in diameter in the center of the bottom. Cut the wick so it's about 50% longer than the can. Draw the wick in through the hole. Let it stick out of the bottom, since that will be the top side of the candle. Extend at least as much wick as you want visible on the candle. Tape over the wick and the hole completely with the duct tape. I use several layers of tape and a bit up the side of the can, to prevent leakage.

To hold the wick at the center of the can, lay a piece of skewer over the center of the opening and tape it down well on both sides. Then, stretch the wick and wrap it around the skewer. Firmly tape it to the side of the can.

When the wax has melted and is about 160°F (70°C), it's time to mold. Slowly pour the melted wax down into the mold in a steady stream.

If you're worried about leakage, pour in only a little at the beginning and let it start hardening before you pour in the rest. Fill the mold until it is ¼ in. (0.5 cm) below the top edge. One tip for guaranteeing a spill-free pour is to place the can in a container filled with an inch or so (a few centimeters) of lukewarm water. The water should not go higher than half the height of the mold, maximum. When you pour the melted wax, the water around the mold will keep it from leaking if there are any small outflows.

A molded candle should harden slowly for best results and to prevent any air bubbles. When you see it beginning to harden, when there's a thin, solid cake on top of the mold, make a couple of holes with a skewer and pour in a little more wax. I usually do this two or three times. If you notice the casting sinking in, you can also fill it in with some melted wax afterward.

After these small steps, all you have to do is wait for the wax to harden completely. I usually let a casting stand either overnight or for a complete workday, about eight hours. That way, the wax will have solidified completely and shrunk in somewhat, which will make it easier to remove from the mold. The easiest way to get the candle out of the mold is to cut away the metal. You can also try removing the candle while leaving the mold intact, but you risk cutting the candle on the sharp can edges.

Cut to the wick on the top and bottom edges. If there are blemishes on the casting that you want to fix, use a knife heated in hot water or use a hairdryer. You can also cut the bottom to even it out.

Casting in a Juice Pouch

Anything can be a casting mold! Casting in a juice pouch, saved from your trash, yields fun and sometimes unexpected results.

WHAT YOU NEED

- Wax mixture (see page 21)
- Kitchen scale
- Melting pot
- Saucepan
- Thermometer
- Wick
- Large-eyed (tapestry) needle
- Empty juice pouch
- Scissors
- Duct tape
- Wooden skewer or a similar little stick to tie wick to

Melt the wax, following instructions on page 21.

Cut off the top off the juice pouch. Use the needle to thread the wick through the center of the bottom, leaving an inch or so (a few centimeters) of wick sticking out from the bottom. Tape over the wick completely with the duct tape to prevent leakage.

Center the wick with a skewer or stick. When the wax has heated to about 160°F (70°C), it's time to mold. It is best to do this in a water bath to minimize the risk of leakage (see page 76). Slowly pour the melted wax down into the mold in a steady stream. Fill the mold until it is ¼ in. (0.5 cm) below the top edge. When you see it beginning to harden, when there's a thin, solid cake on top of the mold, poke a couple of holes with a skewer and pour in a little more melted wax. I usually do this two or three times. If you notice the casting sinking in, you can also fill it in with some melted wax afterward.

Let the casting harden, overnight or for about eight hours. Remove the tape and cut away the juice pouch once the candle has solidified completely. Trim the wick on the top and bottom edges. To fix blemishes on the casting, use a knife heated in hot water or by a hairdryer. You can also trim the bottom to even it out.

Casting in a Toilet Paper Tube

Using toilet paper tubes for crafts is not just for preschoolers. The tube is a perfect form for casting a small block candle.

WHAT YOU NEED

- Wax mixture (see page 21)
- Kitchen scale
- Melting pot
- Saucepan
- Thermometer
- Wick
- Empty toilet paper tube
- A small piece of cardboard, about 2 × 2 in. (5 × 5 cm)
- Hot glue (hot melt adhesive)
- Scissors
- Wooden skewer or a similar little stick to tie wick to
- Duct tape

Melt the wax, following instructions on page 21.

Glue the toilet paper tube to the cardboard. ensuring no gaps. Make a little hole in the cardboard piece, centered on the tube, and draw the wick inside, leaving an inch or so (a few centimeters) of wick sticking out from the bottom. Tape over the wick completely with the duct tape to prevent leakage.

Center the wick with a skewer or stick. When the wax has melted completely, take the melting pot out of the water bath and let it cool somewhat, without letting the wax begin to harden. This is so the wax will harden more quickly in the mold and not seep out through the cardboard. Slowly pour the melted wax into the mold in a steady stream. Fill the mold until it is ¼ in. (0.5 cm) below the top edge. When you see it beginning to harden, follow the directions on page 79 to make two holes.

Let the casting harden, overnight or for about eight hours. Make a little cut in the toilet paper tube and pull the cardboard away from the finished candle.

Trim the wick on the top and bottom edges. You can also trim the bottom to even it out.

Silicone Casting Molds

Casting with an item from nature—for example, a rock—can yield terrific results. Silicone captures the smallest little details, as does the wax, letting you obtain an exact copy of your original item. It takes some preparation, but it's not as hard as you might expect. When making the mold, I use liquid silicone that I pour into a container (such as a yogurt container), with the object firmly attached to the bottom. There are also versions of silicone with a thicker consistency that you can brush on, a good alternative for larger shapes. In this section, I'll teach you the method for using liquid silicone. For this project we'll use a rock, but there are plenty of items in nature you can mold with, such as a piece of a branch, a fruit, or a cone. If you use something that might shift (everything but a rock), you need to anchor it more securely in the jar. A screw or glue usually works well. If you use glue, make sure that the glue works on the material you're using.

WHAT YOU NEED

- Rock or item you want to cast
- A container for the rock, such as a yogurt container. The container shouldn't be too big; the rock needs only about ¾ inch (a couple of centimeters) of space around it. Otherwise, it takes much more of the expensive silicone to make the mold.
- Silicone for casting; you can buy this in hobby shops
- Plaster bandage strips or air-drying clay to cover up any unevenness on the bottom of the rock—and to hold the rock in place during casting
- Kitchen scale
- A container for blending the silicone in, such as a large paper cup or an empty milk carton
- Stirrer

Before you buy silicone, measure to find out how much you need. Silicone is rather expensive, so you don't want to buy or mix more than necessary. A good way to measure is to use stearin flakes as a placeholder for the silicone. Put the rock you want to cast in the container you'll use for casting, and fill the container (with the rock still in it) with stearin flakes up to the top. Then pour the stearin flakes out into a container for measuring, so you can check the volume. Silicone weighs about 126 g per 0.42 cup (1 dL). If the stearin flakes in your container measured 2.75 cups (6.5 dL), you'll need 819 g of silicone to fill it.

Most often, I use a silicone that can be mixed 10 to 1 with hardener. If you need a total of 819 g silicone, you'll actually use about 745 g silicone and 74.5 g hardener. Read the materials packaging to see what proportions it recommends for the mix.

Before you can cast the rock, you need to make sure it's securely attached in the container in the position you want for the candle. It's best if the rock for casting has a relatively flat bottom, so it will remain steady. You might want to have a support base for the rock, partly to anchor it well on its bottom so it won't move during casting, and partly to make sure that cavities won't develop and let the silicone seep in. The easiest way to make a base is with air-drying clay or plaster bandaging.

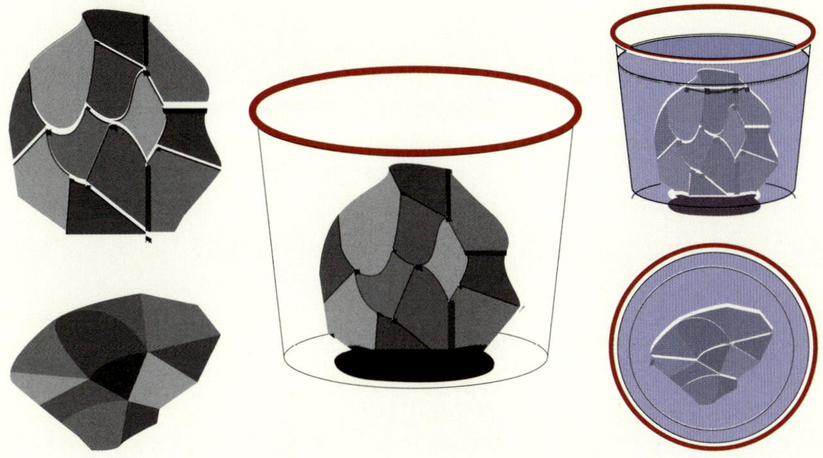

Build up the material until the space between the rock and container is tight and even. Check to ensure that the rock is stable in the container; if not, you can add a little extra material so that the rock has a very stable base. Once the support of clay or plaster is completely dry, it's time to mix the silicone. Mix following your product's instructions. Stir it well for a few minutes so the hardener is evenly distributed. Slowly pour the silicone in an even stream into the container. Cover the rock completely with about an inch (a few centimeters) of silicone. If you happen to spill any silicone, let it harden completely, so it will come off easily.

The amount of time needed for hardening varies depending on which hardener and which silicone you used, so read the package instructions to see what to expect. Once the silicone has hardened, it's time to cut up your mold. It's easiest to begin by cutting off the bottom of the container. Then cut the container up the side so you can pull it away completely. To take the rock out of the mold, you need to cut the silicone. Begin at the bottom of the rock and cut in a zigzag until you reach the top of the rock. If you cut zigzag rather than straight, it will be easier for the mold to return to its original shape. Now you can pry the mold off and pry the rock out. Silicone is quite durable, so don't be afraid of it!

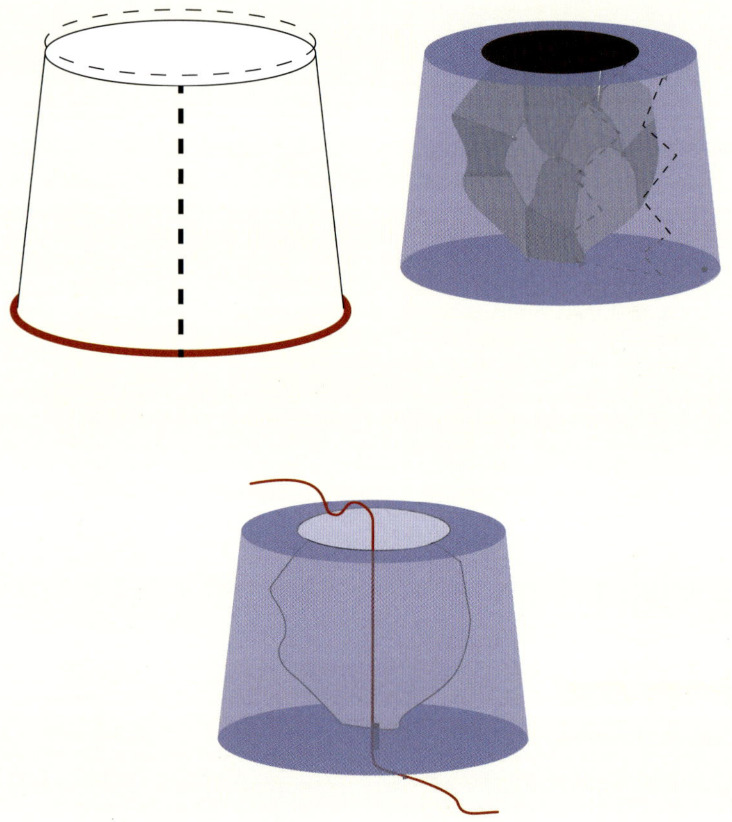

Some types of silicone can be hardened in the oven for a few hours. Check to see if the silicone you have requires that. Your mold is now almost ready to use for casting! The only thing left is to make a hole for the wick. If you have a large-eyed needle, you can use that; otherwise, you can poke a hole with the pointed tip of a skewer. Use the same tool to make the hole and to push the wick in.

When you cast in a silicone form, you need to secure or tighten the form so the wax will stay in the mold and not run out. A strap, steel wire, or strong cord all work well. Test by strapping the mold and filling it with water to make sure it's tight.

3D-Printed Mold

If you're adept at 3-D printing or curious about trying it out, this is a really cool application for the technique. Of course, you can also use a mold design that you download! Thanks to silicone's softness, many complex shapes can be cast with exactly the same technique as I described for the previous project.

I model in Rhinoceros, but there are many different programs that work well. I'm no expert at 3-D printing, but there are instructions on the internet. You'll also need access to a 3-D printer, filament, and materials used for printing.

You can decide if you want layer-on-layer texture to be visible on the finished candle. That can be a great detail! Or, if you want a smooth candle, you can adjust the printer to get as even a surface as possible. It's also excellent to spackle and to sand on a 3-D-printed object.

Once you have a print that you want to cast in silicone, follow the same process I described for the previous project, except for attaching the form to the bottom of your container. With a 3-D print, it's easiest either to glue with a glue suitable for plastic, or to screw it on. Good luck with modeling!

DYEING

Color is a big part of the exploration for me. How color interacts with a form is such an important and exciting part of the expression regarding all forms, and, of course, candles. You can add color to candles in so many different ways. In this chapter, I give a few examples of how using wax and pigment can make a solidly dyed candle, how you can dye the wick, how to cast different-colored candles in layers, and how to bring forth effects such as marbling.

You can buy candle pigment in hobby shops. It's usually a bit expensive, but a little goes a long way. If you have any wax crayons at home, you can try dyeing wax with them—just break off a little and let them melt in your wax.

Handmade candles are lovely in groups, and I often think of that when I'm deciding which colors to use. Using a range of three to five colors is rewarding for creating a nice unity in a group of candles. I can immerse myself in this for a long time . . . blending pigments, making color tests, comparing shades, building up a color world to explore.

1. Bleached beeswax and stearin dyed with light-blue pigment
2. Natural beeswax and stearin dyed with brown pigment
3. Natural beeswax and stearin dyed with red pigment
4. Natural beeswax and stearin dyed with green and brown pigment

3.
4.

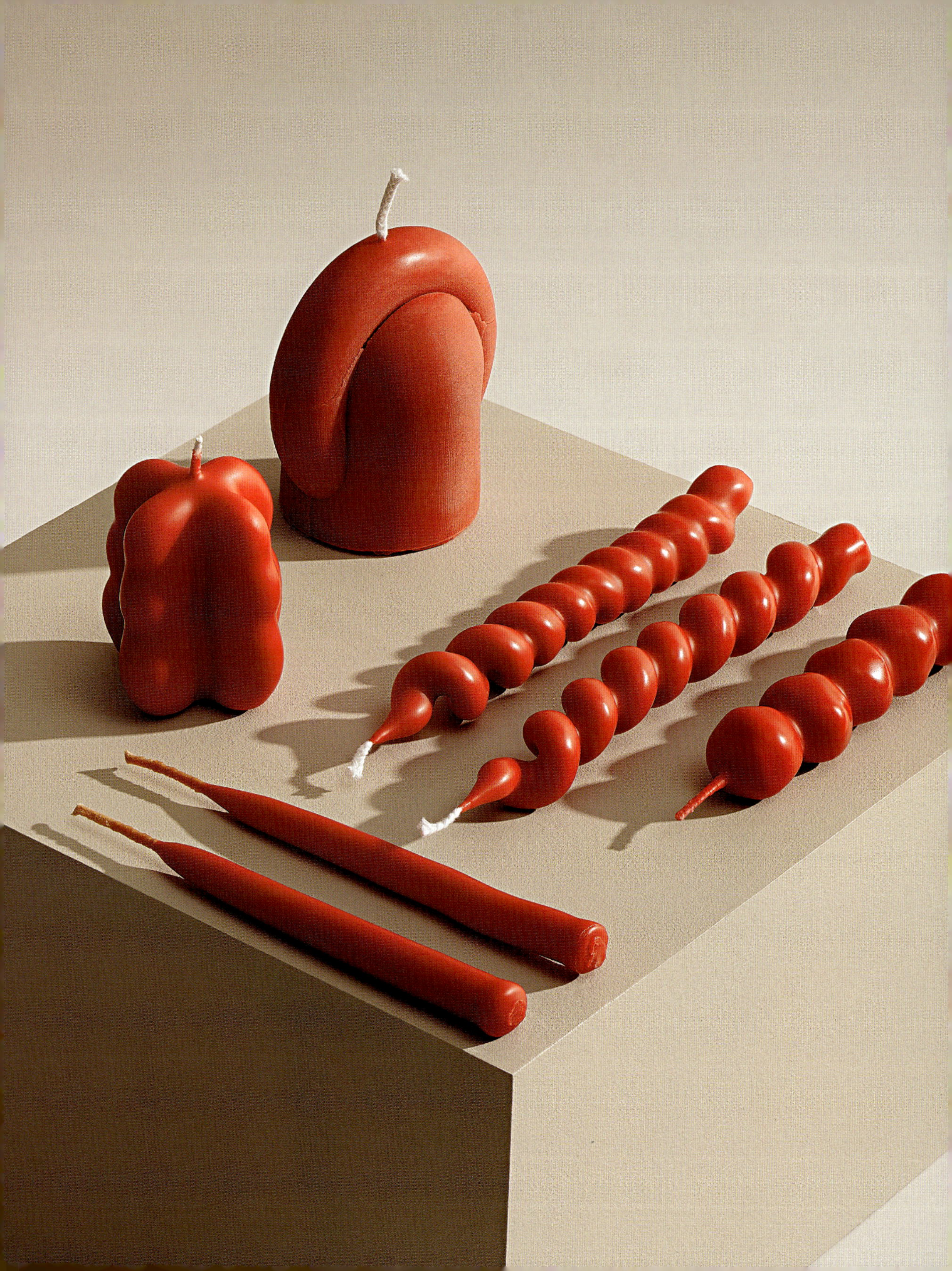

Dyeing Wax with Pigment

Dyeing wax with candle pigment isn't a specialized art and is really mostly about testing for the color you want. The golden-yellow color of natural beeswax is a good base for many colors. However, if you want to blend in a warmer blue or light pastels, it's best to use a colorless wax blend as a base. When using bleached, completely white beeswax, mix it in your wax blend in the same proportions you use with natural beeswax.

WHAT YOU NEED

- Wax mixture (see page 21)
- Dye pigment or wax crayons
- Melting pot
- Saucepan
- Thermometer

Melt the wax, following the instructions on page 21.

When the wax mixture has melted completely, blend the pigment into the wax. Stir the pigment thoroughly into the wax, so the pigment melts completely and is evenly mixed in. Keep in mind that when the wax is in melted form, it is difficult to see what the color of the wax will be, so test the color each time you add pigment. Dip a spoon that has been in the freezer for a while into the wax—the wax should harden immediately on the cold spoon. Let the wax continue to cool for a while; the color will change once the wax has completely cooled.

As always, it's a good idea to think about what pot to use for melting wax and blending in various dyes. Consider what amount you'll need of the color you are mixing—if you're mixing for a specific color, it's disappointing, for example, if there isn't enough when you are in the middle of casting. I usually work with about five colors at a time, so I have a separate pot for each color that I refill when beginning each.

The two dyed candles to the right were made with a combination of techniques. To begin with, before dipping the candles, I dipped the wick in dyed wax. The candle was then dipped in a contrast color of dyed wax. To enjoy flea market candleholder finds in a new way, I centered the candle hanging in the holder and then poured melted wax (the same color as wick was dipped in) into the candleholder. So much more color and shape joy than using plain old tealights in these holders.

Layer-on-Layer Casting

You can make multicolor candles in several different ways. Here's a technique for casting different colors in layers.

WHAT YOU NEED

- Wax mixture (see page 21)
- Dye pigment or wax crayons
- Kitchen scale
- Melting pot
- Saucepan
- Thermometer
- Wick
- Soda can or another type of mold
- Scissors
- Knife
- Screwdriver with small-diameter bit
- Duct tape
- Wooden skewer or similar small stick for tying wick to

Melt the wax, following the instructions on page 21, and prepare the mold (see page 75). Use as many dipping pots as you have colors for your candle. Once the wax is completely melted, mix in your colors, using pigment or wax crayons.

If you want precisely the same thickness in the layers for each of the different colors, work like this: Place your mold on a digital kitchen scale and tare the weight. Fill the mold with water. The amount of water filling the mold can be divided by the number of layers you want to cast. Keep the mold on the scale when you cast the layers, making sure that each layer is the same weight. If you don't intend for all the layers to be the same thickness, you can skip the weighing and pour the wax in freehand.

Each layer needs to harden somewhat before you pour in the next. When there is a hardened cake, about ¼ in. (6 mm), on top that holds its shape when you tap it lightly, it has hardened enough. Once you've cast all the layers, let the mold cool thoroughly, preferably overnight, before you remove the casting.

Dip Painting in a Water Bath

This technique achieves interesting effects. You can dip-paint both dipped and molded creations.

WHAT YOU NEED

- A saucepan half filled with water
- Melted wax or pigment
- Finished dipped or molded candle

Heat the water in the saucepan to about 160°F (70°C). Pour a little melted wax into the water. It will lie on the surface of the water and maintain its liquid form. If the wax hardens when you pour it into the water, the water needs to be hotter. To use use pigment for a dip painting, pour some pigment flakes into the water and let them melt.

Experiment with using various colors to separate or mix for marbling. You can use a skewer and carefully mix different colors so they move together and create striking patterns.

Then, all you have to do is dip the candle in the water. Dip the candle quickly, so it doesn't begin melting in the hot water. Test the results from dipping the candle in both straight down and at an angle. Spin, twist, and turn the candle while you dip it for a variety of effects.

When you're finished dipping, let the water cool down completely, so the wax hardens and will be easy to pick out and reuse.

Marbleized Block Candle

You'll cast this candle a little differently. Lay several wicks in a row on a mold and cut the candles out once the block has hardened. A square can or baking pan works well as a mold—a square silicone baking pan is perfect. A pan that's a maximum size of 11¾ × 8 in. (30 × 20 cm) is fine—larger than that and you'd need a lot of wax. Marbling is best with two or three colors; otherwise, there is a risk of producing a meat-colored mess. Take it from someone who knows!

WHAT YOU NEED

- Wax mixture (see page 21)
- Dye pigment or wax crayons
- Kitchen scale
- Melting pot
- Saucepan
- Thermometer
- Wick
- Scissors
- Mold to cast in
- Knife, preferably a utility knife
- Steel ruler
- Hot-air gun or hot water
- Tape

Melt the wax in three separate melting pots, following the instructions on page 21. Dye the wax with pigment or wax crayons until you are happy with the colors.

Cut the wicks somewhat longer than the length of the mold you will cast in. When the wax has melted and you are happy with the colors, you can begin casting. Do a three-part pour: Pour a little of one color into the mold, change to the second color, and then add the third. Let the wax begin to cool but barely harden, before you do your next three-part pour. Continue to alternately pour the colors in until the wax is ⅜–⅝ in. (1–1.5 cm) thick in the mold—let it harden a little more this time, until it begins forming a hardened cake on top. Lay the wicks evenly spaced in the wax. Don't forget that the candles on each end will be about 1¼ in. (3 cm) wide. The total number of candles you can fit in depends on how wide they are. Tape the ends of the wicks securely to the mold, so they will stay in place as you continue molding.

When the wax has hardened more, you can continue with the second half of your casting. Alternately pour on the various colors until the wicks are completely covered with ¾ in. (2 cm) of wax. Let the wax cool completely, eight hours at minimum. Now you have several wicks molded into a marbled block, ideally with a nice pattern visible. Now it's time to cut out the candles. Take the casting out of the mold and lay it on a cutting mat or other protective surface. Heat the knife up well—either with a hairdryer or by holding it in hot water for a while—so it will be easier to cut through the block. Cut out the candles, using the steel ruler as a cutting edge so they'll be straight. Or cut them into more-organic shapes—maybe half circles?

IDEAS AND EXPERIMENTS

The many possibilities of wax are truly inspiring! And the other great thing? Since you can always melt down your mistakes, there's no reason not to try out your ideas.

There are many contemporary candlemakers who work with wax in innovative and exciting ways, plus the many timeless traditional candle ideas that have developed around the world. You can learn from them all. This chapter could be endlessly long, but instead I've collected just a few projects that I think show the possibilities of the material and that inspire me to keep exploring.

1. Wax vase
2. Experiment with textile and wax
3. Birthday cake candles
4. Wax candlestick holders
5. Casting in sand

4.
5.

Casting in Sand

This is an exciting project that I think would be fun to make on a beach, but it's great for making at home too. A perfect project to work on with children, it's quick and you get to dig in the sand—the kids will like that! The mold can be almost anything you want; try a rock, the bottom of a bottle, or a small toy. You can also sculpt a shape with your hands.

WHAT YOU NEED

- Sand (sand from the pet store, sandbox sand, or sand from the beach)
- A can or container to put the sand in
- Item to make impression in the sand
- Spray bottle with water
- Wax mixture (see page 21)
- Dye pigment or wax crayons
- Kitchen scale
- Melting pot
- Saucepan
- Thermometer
- Wick
- Scissors
- Tape
- Wooden skewers or similar stick for centering wick

Melt the wax, following the instructions on page 21. Pour the sand into the can and spray it with water. The sand should be quite damp. Depending on the item you'll be casting, you can either place it in the can and then press the sand around it, or first press the sand down evenly into the can and then push the object to be molded into the sand to make an impression.

When you have the impression, make a hole for the wick in the middle of the form with the pointed end of a skewer, all the way down to the bottom of the can. To make it easier to set the wick in the hole, you can first dip it in wax and let it harden. Place the wick in the hole, then lay a skewer over the can's opening and secure it with a piece of tape. Twist the top end of the wick around the skewer and tape it into place.

When the wax has melted completely, it's time for casting. Slowly pour the melted wax into the sand mold. Let the cast harden completely before you remove it. Gently pull on the wick to loosen the cast. Carefully pull up the cast so you can use the same sand mold again.

Brush off the candle and trim the wick on the underside. If necessary, cut away any unevenness on the bottom of the candle so it can sit upright and steady.

Wax Candlestick Holder

Here's an object that takes wax a step away from its original function of flameholder. Let freedom take the lead as you shape a candleholder: It can be high or low, hold one or more candles, and, of course, feature different colors.

WHAT YOU NEED

- Beeswax sheet (whole or leftovers)
- Wax mixture (see page 21)
- Wooden skewers
- A candle to use for shaping the holder
- Melting pot
- Saucepan
- Thermometer

Melt the wax mixture, following the instructions on page 21.

Begin building your candleholder with small pieces of beeswax sheet. Use a candle you want to put in the holder as a template for an appropriate size for the holder. Manipulate and sculpt the wax until it's a shape you're happy with.

To dip the holder without a wick to hold on to, you can use a skewer. Stick the pointed end of the skewer into the holder, preferably someplace where a little mark won't be seen (for example, the inside bottom of the holder or the underside of its base). With the wax candlestick impaled on the skewer, you can hold it as you dip.

Dip until the beeswax sheet is no longer visible. Use a knife to cut away any drips from the bottom. Make sure the candlestick stands steady on its own and with a candle in it before you use it. Keep an eye on any candle while it's burning, and in this case, don't let the candle burn down completely in its wax candleholder.

Birthday Cake Candles

Birthday cake candles are really just small tapers that can capture all our wishes. They're easy and quick to make, and the cake will be a hundred times better with homemade candles. Making the rolled beeswax variation is even quicker than running out to the store to buy candles!

WHAT YOU NEED

- Wax mixture (see page 21)
- Pigment or wax crayons
- Kitchen scale
- Melting pot
- Saucepan
- Thermometer
- Wick
- Scissors
- Knife
- Wooden skewers or similar small stick for tying wick to
- A place to hang the skewer with candles while they dry (for example, between two chairs or book stacks)

ROLLED BEESWAX VARIATION

- Beeswax sheet (whole or leftovers)
- Wick
- Scissors

Melt the wax, following the instructions on page 21, using as many pots as you have candle colors. When the wax has melted, dye it with pigment or wax crayons until you are happy with the color(s).

Cut the wicks longer than the length of the candles you want to make. Securely tie the wicks to a skewer.

If you want to dye the wick in a contrasting color, begin by dipping it in colored wax. Straighten out the wicks once you've finished dipping but while they are still warm.

Then dip the wick into the wax and let it cool between each dip. Straighten out the candle now and then if it gets crooked. A birthday cake candle needs fewer dips than a regular taper. When the candle is a shape you like, cut away any drips from the bottom of the candle and let it cool completely.

For the rolled beeswax birthday cake candles shown on the facing page, work this way: Cut the wicks the length of the candles you want to make. Take small pieces of beeswax sheet and press and roll them firmly on the wick until the candles are a shape you are happy with. Done!

Wax Vase

Wax can actually do other things than holding a flame—it can also hold water. To make this vase, I started with a beeswax base and then dipped it. To learn the process, begin with a small vase. As they get larger, vases can collapse under their own weight—creating amazing, baggy shapes like the one shown on the facing page.

WHAT YOU NEED

- Beeswax sheets
- Knife
- Wax mixture (see page 21)
- Melting pot
- Saucepan
- Thermometer
- Cutting mat or other protective surface

Melt the wax, following the instructions on page 21. Use a melting pot that is big enough to fit the size of vase you want. Cut up the beeswax sheets and begin shaping them as you want for your vase. Use several layers of beeswax, at least two. If it's too thin, the vase can easily collapse when the wax heats up during dipping. Take your inspiration from ceramic techniques: Cut out a shape that you can bend into a cylinder, or try rolling a sheet up into a ring. Attach the sheets to each other by pinching them together with your fingers. They'll melt together well when you dip them.

When you have a shape you're happy with, it's time for dipping. Make sure the form is cohesive enough that it won't fall apart when you dip it. Hold the vase and dip as far down into the wax as you can. Let it cool a little before you turn it, holding the other end of the vase and dipping it in the other direction. To ensure that the vase will become watertight, pour melted wax into the vase and let it harden somewhat along the bottom and sides of the vase before you pour the excess out. If you notice that it leaks in some places, you can patch it with beeswax sheet before you dip it some more. If you're making a larger vase, let it cool well between each dip, so as to avoid having it collapse under its own weight when the material becomes warm and soft.

You can also take advantage of the material's softness for shaping a vase—for example, if you want to shape a baggy vase like the one shown on page 120 or even it out in some other way, you can adjust the shape as you dip. Dip the vase until you're satisfied with the shape. Cut away any irregularities on the bottom. Make sure the vase sits evenly and is watertight before you let it cool completely.

You can experiment with both the shape and color of vases. I colored the vase shown at right with dip painting—see the instructions on page 101. For it, I used blue pigment that I crumbled into the water bath.

Project Index

Anna Dykhoff is a set designer and interior designer working primarily in film, television, and the performing arts. Her design curiosity led her to try working with wax as a potential set-creation medium, and then she decided to make a few candles. What started as a quick experiment in the kitchen has now expanded to a workshop, formerly known as her garage. She teaches her striking candle design techniques to makers of all kinds. Anna holds a degree in interior architecture and furniture design from Konstfack University of Arts, Crafts and Design. Instagram: @annadykhoff